I0751117

CYNTHIA ROTHROCK

ROTHROCK 'N' ROLL WITH THE PUNCHES

Library of Congress Cataloging-In-Publication Data
Rothrock, Cynthia Ann

Cynthia Rothrock
p.cm

ISBN: 978-0-9859395-6-4

Summary: In *Rothrock 'n' Roll with the Punches: Surviving Hong Kong Action Cinema*, martial arts legend Cynthia Rothrock delivers a gripping, behind-the-scenes look at her groundbreaking journey as one of the few Western women to break into the high-octane world of 1980s and '90s Hong Kong film industry. With raw honesty and infectious energy, Rothrock shares the triumphs and bruises—both literal and figurative—of training with top stunt teams, navigating a male-dominated industry, and earning respect in a culture where she was often the outsider.
Packed with behind the scenes stories, cultural clashes, and adrenaline-fueled set moments, this memoir is an inspiring testament to perseverance, passion, and the power of kicking down doors—on and off screen.

FIRST EDITION

For more information about permission to reproduce selections from this book, email: cynthiarothrockofficial@outlook.com

Book Design: SpiralShare Marketing
https://marketing.spiralshare.com

This book is dedicated to my beautiful daughter, Skyler,
my amazing mom, Joy, my wonderful parter, Robert,
and to all my fans around the world.

FOREWORD BY SCOTT ADKINS

I still remember the first time I met Cynthia Rothrock. I was just a teenager—wide-eyed, full of dreams, and completely obsessed with martial arts films. I was so impressed by her agility and power for such a petite little blonde American girl, and to see her move with more grace and more power than the men was awe-inspiring. She was already a star, a trailblazer who had conquered the Hong Kong action scene and become a household name for fans like me. When I nervously approached her at an event, she didn't just smile and sign an autograph—she wrote a message that stuck with me for years: "See you in the movies." At the time, it felt like a kind gesture, maybe even a polite encouragement to a young fan. But for me, it became a prophecy. Those words lit a fire in me. Years later, when I saw her again—this time at the London Comicon—it hit me just how much Cynthia had influenced my path.

Cynthia's story isn't just about kicks and punches—it's about courage, resilience, and breaking barriers. What she accomplished in the gritty, high-pressure world of Hong Kong cinema was unprecedented, especially for a woman in an industry that didn't exactly roll out the red carpet. This book is a raw, fascinating look at that journey—from the inside.

If you've ever wondered what it takes to not only survive but thrive in a world where every move counts, Cynthia lays it all out here with the same honesty and intensity she brings to every fight scene.

I'm honored to write this foreword, because her legacy isn't just in the films we watch—it's in the dreams she ignites in all of us who dare to step into the world of martial arts action movies!

~Scott Adkins

See you in the movies
Love, Cynthia

CONTENTS

CHAPTER 1

THE ACCIDENTAL ACTION STAR

"Perseverance isn't about never failing—it's about rising every time, stronger, wiser, and more determined to finish what you started. The real fight is in never giving up."

I never set out to become a movie star. In fact, acting wasn't even on my radar. When my film career got started, I was focused on teaching martial arts, running my school, and competing professionally. That was my world. That was my passion.

Martial arts didn't come into my life with a bang—it snuck into my life quietly, when I was a 13-year-old growing up in Scranton, Pennsylvania. I remember stepping into the *Scranton Karate Studio* for the first time at the invitation of my friend. It wasn't love at first workout. Not even close. There were very few women training, and absolutely none teaching or competing at the highest levels. I was intimidated. Honestly questioned if I even belonged there.

Each class seemed more brutal than the last—nothing like the structured, supportive environments you see today. There weren't kids' classes or trial lessons or glossy ads. It was raw. It was tough. The mentality was simple: survive the class, or don't come back. It was sink or swim, and I felt like I was drowning.

I was constantly getting hurt, physically exhausted, and emotionally overwhelmed. I came home one day in tears and told my mom I was done, that martial arts just wasn't for me. But she wouldn't let me quit. She told me I had to finish what I started, even if it was hard. She also added I signed a four month contract and had to at least do that. Not long after that, I was in class when my instructor stopped everything and had us all sit against the wall, and began a short lecture in which he said, "Quitters are losers." I don't know if he was actually talking to me—but it felt like he was staring right through me when he said it. That moment stuck with me. I made a quiet promise to myself that I wouldn't be a quitter… and I definitely wasn't going to be a loser.

With my improved mindset, I watched a demonstration with new eyes—clean, sharp, powerful. The movement was so precise, so fluid, so fierce… it felt like watching poetry in motion. That was it. Something inside me lit up. I knew I had to learn how to move like that.

Five months into my training, I entered my first competition. There was a women's division, but no rank or belt separation. Just one division. So I competed against black belts—and I ranked second among them. That victory changed everything for me. I thought, "If I can beat black belts now, I'm going all the way. I'm going to strive to be the best."

I competed in New Jersey at an A-Rated tournament with the best of the best and took first place. Everyone was saying I should compete professionally.

So, I made a decision: I'd compete for five years professionally, strive to be undefeated, and retire ranked number one, because I thought it'd be a record that would be hard to beat.

What started as curiosity quickly became an obsession. I trained relentlessly, pushing myself every single day. I studied multiple disciplines—Tang Soo Do, Taekwondo, Northern Shaolin, Eagle Claw, Wushu, and more. I wasn't interested in being just good—I wanted to be the best. I worked hard at it. That became my world.

I competed almost every weekend—sometimes twice a week. I trained like a machine. In those five years, I was undefeated in over 500 competitions across forms and weapons. And I didn't just stay local—I took my training global. I went to Mainland China in the '80s, and trained in Hong Kong and Taiwan, immersing myself in the roots of the styles I loved. I wasn't just chasing trophies. I was chasing mastery.

"Looking back, I didn't know exactly where all of it would lead. But I knew one thing—I wasn't going to let anything stop me."

By the early 1980s, I was competing professionally and winning. Between 1981 and 1985, I held five World Championships in forms and weapons. Not just among women—overall. That meant going up against the top male martial artists.

In 1982 I was rated number one in weapons in North America by *Karate Illustrated* magazine. It was unheard of that a woman bested men in those divisions.

It was an amazing time. My life was packed with travel, tournaments, and teaching. I moved myself to California to join the elite *West Coast Demonstration Team*, led by Ernie Reyes, which was known across the country for its high-energy, cutting-edge performances. We'd perform choreographed martial arts routines, including weapons work and self-defense sequences, at major events and martial arts expos. We were tight, like a family, and the best of the best.

Then one day, everything changed.

Ernie got a phone call from the editor of *Kung Fu* magazine that a production company in Hong Kong was looking for the next Bruce Lee—a charismatic martial artist who could carry action films. The producers had scouted all over Asia but hadn't found what they were looking for, so they decided to check out the American scene. Although they were mainly interested in male martial artists, they were open to seeing women too, just in case. Ernie told a few of us on the team about the audition, and we figured, why not? It sounded like fun.

I didn't think much of it when I walked into that audition. I wasn't nervous. I didn't feel like I was trying to win a part—I just wanted to show what I could do. I performed some of my best forms, both empty-hand self defense and weapons. At one point I was going hard with my hook swords and clipped the ceiling with plaster raining down on me. The school owner wasn't too happy that I was ripping up his school, but I just continued and showcased my speed, power, and flexibility. I demonstrated self-defense moves, blending traditional techniques with flashy performance flair. I was doing what I always did.

Afterward, I noticed a small group of men talking quietly at the back of the room. One of them was Corey Yuen, a well-known director and producer from Hong Kong. I later learned that after watching my performance, he turned to the others and said, "Forget the guys—I want the girl."

And just like that, my life took a completely unexpected turn.

"Looking back, it feels like fate. I didn't plan for any of this. I wasn't chasing fame or the movie industry. I just followed my passion, stayed true to my craft, and gave every performance every ounce of everything I had."

In June 1985, I was on a plane to Hong Kong to film my first action movie. I had no acting experience, didn't speak the language, and had never been on a movie set. But I was ready to fight—and I knew how to move. That first film was *Yes, Madam!*, and I starred alongside the amazing Michelle Yeoh. We didn't know it at the time, but that movie would become a cult classic and spark a whole new era of female-led martial arts cinema in Asia.

The rest? That was destiny kicking in. And that's how I became an action star—*by accident.*

CHAPTER 2

HAN'S ISLAND

"Your greatest growth comes when you step beyond the box, into the unknown—where the rules are different, the challenges are real, and every step forward shapes the warrior you're meant to become."

Flying into Hong Kong for the first time felt like something straight out of a movie—literally. As the plane descended, weaving between mountains and gliding over the harbor, I remember looking out the window and thinking, This looks exactly like Han's Island from *Enter the Dragon.* The jagged coastline, the dense city packed with high-rise buildings, the mist curling over the hills—it was surreal. I'd grown up watching a few of the old Chinese martial arts flicks and a Bruce Lee movie or two, never imagining that one day I'd be flying into the heart of martial arts cinema to star in one of my own.

When I landed in June 1985, I didn't know what to expect. In my mind, I was just a martial artist from

Scranton with a U.S. passport and a suitcase full of karate uniforms.

To make things even more unexpected, I had originally pictured myself playing a traditional Chinese-style fighter—something out of a period film, maybe with long flowing robes, dramatic fight scenes, and razors hidden in my braided hair. That's honestly what I thought I was flying out there for. But when I arrived and saw the script, I found out I'd be playing Inspector Carrie Morris from Scotland Yard—a tough, modern-day cop with a badge, a gun, and a whole lot of attitude. It completely threw me. I remember thinking, Wait… I'm not going to be a Shaolin warrior? I'm a British police officer?

And then, just to add to the whirlwind, a massive monsoon hit Hong Kong almost immediately after I arrived.

Suddenly, I was stuck in my hotel room with nothing to do—no television, no English newspapers, no one to talk to. I didn't even have a phone I could use to call home. It was just me, the four walls, and the sound of rain pounding against the windows. The excitement of being in a foreign country quickly turned into a bad case of cabin fever. I remember pacing the room, shadowboxing just to burn off energy, wondering if I'd made a huge mistake. *What am I doing here?* I thought. *This wasn't part of the plan.* But little did I know, everything was about to change—and fast.

This whole experience turned out to be the perfect role to launch my film career. Sometimes the biggest changes—like flying into the unexpected—are the ones that open doors you never even knew existed. You just have to be brave enough to walk through them.

CHAPTER 3

YES, MADAM!

"Sometimes the most unexpected paths lead to the most unforgettable rewards. Trust your journey—life's detours can turn you into someone stronger than you ever imagined."

My very first scene ever on *Yes, Madam*—my big debut—was at the Hong Kong airport, and to this day, it's still one of my favorite scenes. You know the one: I come charging in wearing heels and a dress, like it's just another Tuesday, elbows and kicks flying, ready to take down bad guys.

I was working with Eddie Maher, who was the unfortunate soul getting knocked around by me. Poor Eddie—he's dressed in a tank top, no pads, no protection, just raw bravery *(or maybe a lapse in judgment)*. I had to throw an elbow at him and of course, I'm trying to be careful not to injure him—it's my first scene! Meanwhile, director Corey Yuen is yelling, *"Harder, Cyndi! Hit harder!"* and Eddie's behind me whispering, *"Oh God, please don't hit any harder, you're killing me."* So there I am, caught between a director wanting realism, and an actor wanting to survive. I had no idea what to do—smash or save?

Then came the wall jump. There's this moment in the scene where I leap off the wall, swing around mid-air, and land a kick—all while wearing a dress. Not exactly ideal stunt attire. That move took some serious time to get right, especially with the added fun of trying not to flash the entire airport. We were shooting overnight when the airport was closed—we started around midnight and wrapped around five in the morning. It was a long night, and to make things even more fun, I hadn't slept a wink. I was so nervous, I couldn't even close my eyes the night before.

At one point, I must've looked like I was about to pass out, because Mang Hoi comes over, super sweet, and hands me a piece of candy. "Here," he says, "it'll help. It's ginger." What he didn't know—or maybe did—is that I can't stand ginger. I tried to be polite, popped it in my mouth… and instantly regretted it. My face turned green, my eyes bulged out, and Mang Hoi looks at me and says, "You can spit it out." And I did—like I was exorcising a demon. Between the nerves, the no sleep, and the surprise ginger bomb, that first night of shooting was wild.

Girl Power

From the moment I met Michelle Yeoh on the set of *Yes, Madam!*, I knew we were going to click. There was this quiet strength about her—you could tell she was tough as nails underneath it all. We were both new to the action film world, both learning the ropes in this whirlwind of Hong Kong cinema, and instantly found common ground. What could've been a competitive situation turned into an incredible friendship on-set built on mutual respect. We were two women, thrown into this chaotic, male-dominated industry, trying to prove that we belonged—and we did it together, side by side.

Michelle and I trained, rehearsed, laughed, and got bruised together. When one of us got slammed into a wall or took a hit the wrong way, the other was right there—checking in, helping up, sharing a joke to shake it off. We relied on each other—not just for the action beats, but for the emotional support that kept us going. Off-camera, we'd talk about everything: the cultural differences, the insane pace of filming, even the pressure we felt as women leading an action movie in a world where that was practically unheard of. Michelle was—and still is—one of the most hardworking, and generous people I've ever met. We became sisters in the fight, both literally and figuratively.

Michelle and I were 100% on the same page when it came to our fight scenes—we wanted them to look powerful, real, and intense. No pulling punches, no faking it. So there we are, filming the now-famous bathroom fight scene, going full out… without pads. No elbow guards, no knee protection, nothing. Just raw skin, tile floors, and determination. This was only our second fight scene together, and by the end of it, we were both absolutely covered in bruises. I'm talking black and blue like walking human road maps.

The next day, we show up on set and we could barely touch the skin on our arms and legs without wincing. Every time we threw a punch or blocked a kick, we'd flinch—not from the acting, but from the sheer pain of bone-on-bone contact. We were trying so hard not to make faces, but it was impossible. Every hit felt like we were re-bruising the same spot for the hundredth time. That day I learned one of my most valuable lessons in Hong Kong filmmaking: forget about looking cool in short sleeves—wear pads. And if you can't wear pads, wear clothes that cover everything. You'll thank yourself later when you're not limping through the next scene like a zombie.

Language Barrier *(and a Little Blood)*

One of the first things I learned—very quickly—about making movies in Hong Kong is that nothing works the way you think it will. For example: dialogue. I remember getting my script and asking, "How am I going to speak my Cantonese lines?" The crew just kind of looked at me like I'd asked when lunch would be served on the moon. That's when someone casually mentioned, "Oh no, we dub all the dialogue and insert sound later." I was stunned. I thought, Wait… you mean I can say literally anything? Turns out—yes I could.

So, naturally, when it came time to film a scene where I had to speak Cantonese—which, spoiler alert, I absolutely do not—I asked Corey Yuen what I should say. He just waved his hand and told me, "Just move your mouth and mimic your lines." That was the entire direction. So, with zero Cantonese and a lot of nerves, I went for it and just started mouthing my lines in Cantonese them it just came out, "humma humma humma" with intense emotional commitment which made me laugh. Somehow, when they dubbed it later, it actually matched. To this day, I still have fans come up to me and say, "Wow, your Cantonese is so good!" And I just smile and nod, thinking, If only you knew I was basically saying gibberish with confidence.

Language bit me again during the filming of the final fight scene—me vs. Dick Wei. Oh boy. Before we even started filming, all the Hong Kong stunt guys kept coming up to me with these wide-eyed looks, whispering to a translator things like, "Oof… I feel sorry for you," and "He hits everyone hard." Not exactly reassuring. So I'm hyped up, a little nervous, and thinking, Okay, how bad can it really be? Well, turns out… pretty bad. We get into the fight, and sure enough, Dick Wei is hitting me like a freight train. There's one part of the scene where he kicks me right in the groin—and let me tell you, I used to think that kind of pain was a guy-exclusive experience. Nope. It hurts women too. A lot. That was an eye-opener.

Then comes the famous hook kick. The idea was, he kicks, his foot gets stuck on the wall, I move in, and he kicks me off. Clean, controlled, timed and choreographed… in theory. So he kicks, and at that moment, director Corey Yuen, trying to use more

English on set, yells "Cut!". Unfortunately, Dick Wei didn't speak English at all. So I stop like I'm supposed to. *BAM!* He kicks me square in the side of the head. I saw stars and not the glamorous kind—more like the you might be about to black out kind.

My vision went fuzzy, and I started to wobble. Then I felt something warm... blood was coming out of my ear. And I'm thinking, Wait a minute, isn't that what happens when you die? Blood comes out of your ear. Oh no. Am I dying on the set of my first film?!

They rushed me to the hospital, and the doctor looks at me all calm and says, "He kicked you so hard, he split your internal ear. Nothing we can do. Go back to set." Seriously? That was it.

So I'm back on set, with my ear dripping, possibly concussed, and every time Dick Wei lifted his leg I flinched like a cat near a bathtub. I spent the whole rest of the scene convinced I was going to get kicked again—with blood spurting out of my ear in slow motion. It was the first time in my life I almost got knocked out cold *(and it was on camera)*... and it wouldn't be the last time.

Swordplay Slash

Now if getting kicked in the head wasn't enough, let's talk about the sword fight scene. At this point, I'm taking on a small army—eight guys, all swinging swords and other sharp, pointy objects at me. And here's the thing about shooting fight scenes in Hong Kong: they move fast. You've got to remember thirty, sometimes forty moves in a single take, no room for hesitation, no second chances. Blink, and you're getting clocked. And yep—that's exactly what happened. One guy missed his cue and *thwack*—I took a sword dead-center to the nose. My whole face exploded in pain, my eyes started watering like someone turned on a faucet, and my nose swelled up almost instantly. I'm trying to power through, all teary-eyed and wobbly, and Corey walks over, takes one look at me and says, "Oh… your nose looks better now than before." Thanks, Corey. I'm thinking, "Glad my broken face is working for you."

Brick Wall Yoga

There's this one scene in *Yes, Madam!* that still blows my mind every time I watch it. It's an aerial shot—me flying through the air with a bow staff, landing in a full split on a wall. Even today, when I see it, I think, "Oh my God," I actually did that. It looks so cool on screen, but let me tell you—getting that shot was a whole adventure in itself.

It started simple enough… at least in Hong Kong stunt terms. I had to do this aerial move, hit the wall with my foot, and bounce back down. So we did a few takes of that—up, hit the wall, down. Then the stunt team decided to up the ante. They added this teeny little ledge on the wall, just big enough for one toe, and the idea was that I'd plant one foot on the ledge while the other leg was over my head, bow staff in hand, and strike a split pose midair. If you can picture it—I'm balancing on a stick, one foot hanging off into nothing, the other foot cranked sky-high, basically doing yoga on a brick wall.

Now here's where it gets really fun: they drilled two tiny holes in the wall, ran wires through them, strapped me in around the waist, and said, "Okay, when we yell action, your leg goes up, we'll yank you sideways, and you'll go completely horizontal in a split against the wall." I mean, what could go wrong, right?

So they hoist me up, and boom—I'm flatlined against the wall like some kind of human poster. Then they ask, "Do you want to come down between takes, or just stay there?" And me, trying to be tough, thinking, Eh, I can hold a split all day, I go, "I'll stay up."

Bad idea.

I stayed in that split for an hour—strapped to a wall, midair, trying not to let on that I was slowly losing feeling in my legs. I didn't want to be the wimp who cried uncle. But the next day? Oh, I paid for it. I could barely walk. My legs were so sore I looked like I'd just run a marathon in horse stance. But hey—it looked amazing on screen.

The final fight scene in *Yes, Madam!* took over a month to shoot—just that one scene! But wow, was it was amazing. Even now, when I watch it, I'm still blown away by what we pulled off. I remember hearing later that Sylvester Stallone watched that scene with his stunt team. One of his guys told me, "Sly kept asking, 'How do they do this? How is that even possible?'" That was the kind of impact it had. The action wasn't just fast—it was creative, and insane.

The risks of injury were high—it came with the territory. There's a fight scene where a stuntman gets kicked off a glass balcony and falls straight into a fountain of shattered glass. Another stuntman flies off a second story balcony and cracks his back on a wooden bar below before crumpling onto the floor. Fans still ask me, "That had to be a dummy, right?" Nope. That was a real person. And yes, both really did those falls—and yes, both definitely walked away with serious injuries. But that's Hong Kong stunt work for you. These guys were fearless. Hats off to them—every single one of them. Their level of dedication, pain tolerance, and sheer bravery is next-level.

"Filming in Hong Kong taught me fast that you can get seriously hurt—or worse—but the attitude was: don't complain, don't quit, just keep going until you nail it. That was the job."

When we finally wrapped, *Yes, Madam!* became a massive hit in Hong Kong. And me? I thought it would be my only movie. Honestly, I figured, Hey, maybe I'll end up on a poster, maybe someday my future kids will see it and go, "Look—Mom was in a movie!" That's all I expected. But then *Golden Harvest* camc back to me with another offer. "Let's do more." Next thing I knew, I was filming *Shanghai Express* and launching a full-blown action career.

It's wild to think that this movie is over 30 years old now, and people still talk about that final fight. It still holds up—no CGI, no shortcuts, just real martial artists doing real stunts. We had a bit of wire work here and there, but everything else was raw, physical, and absolutely brutal. That's what I loved then, and what I still love now. Even though I'd wake up in Hong Kong thinking, Okay, this is the one where I die, I'd finish the shoot, bandage myself up, and go, So… when's the next one? It was this wild rollercoaster of pain and passion—but man, what a ride.

"That's the thing about making action movies in Hong Kong: you don't just act tough—you become tough. You get hit, you get bruised, you bleed, you keep going."

It was painful, chaotic, and absolutely wild… but I loved every second of it. The film was originally scheduled to shoot in four months. But, surprise! Seven and a half months later, I was still going. I basically lived in Hong Kong at that point. It was exhausting, grueling… and I wouldn't trade a single moment of it. Well, maybe just the bruises.

CHAPTER 4

MILLIONAIRES EXPRESS

(AKA SHANGHAI EXPRESS)

"Life will throw punches, and yes—you'll get a little bruised along the way. But if you can laugh, learn, and keep moving forward, you'll realize the ride is half the adventure, and every bruise is just proof you showed up for it."

Millionaires Express came hot on the heels of *Yes, Madam!*. That movie took off like a rocket, and the next thing I knew, *Golden Harvest* swooped in and signed me to a three-picture deal. Other film studios were interested, but I'd grown up watching Jackie Chan and chose to sign with *Golden Harvest*.

I flew back home for a quick break—maybe three weeks, tops—and thought, *Alright, Cynthia, time to train like a beast and get in the best shape of your life!*

And I did… right up until the moment I blew out my ACL doing a jump spinning hook kick. Yep. I land, feel that dreaded *pop*, and boom—total knee disaster. And what do I do? Naturally, I decided not to tell anyone.

I'm thinking, "I'll just fake it. Tape it up, act tough, and hope no one notices."

Fast forward—I arrive on set (concealing a slight limp), and this is where I meet Richard Norton for the first time. We immediately became friends, mainly because we were among the few people on set who spoke English. It was an instant bond and one that lasted a lifetime.

So, I confide in him. "Richard, I blew out my knee. I don't know if I'm even going to be able to kick." He looks at me with this wide-eyed stare and goes, "No way, mate! I just got back from the Philippines where I got sliced by a bush—and it got infected. My leg blew up like a balloon. They had to drain it three times!"

We just stood there, the two lead fighters of the film, realizing neither of us could currently, you know… fight. We looked at each other like, *What could possibly go wrong?* Richard just says, "We can power through this. Onward and upward." So we did just that.

Just then in walks martial arts actor Hwang Jang-lee who plays Yukio Fushiki in the film. Now, at that time, Richard and I didn't know who he was, but he struts over to us—big smile, confident vibe—and starts chatting. Suddenly, the conversation turns into some kind of martial arts one-upmanship between him and Richard.

It starts simple enough.

Hwang: "Richard, can you do a jumping sidekick?"

Richard: "Yeah, of course, mate."

Hwang: "Well, I can do a jumping sidekick into a jumping inside crescent kick."

Richard: "Oh yeah? Well, I can do a double jumping sidekick, spin mid-air, throw a front kick, do a split in the air, recite Shakespeare, and tie my shoelaces without touching the ground!"

Okay, maybe he didn't say the Shakespeare part and I'm not sure how you don't land your kick, but you get the idea.

I'm standing there, jaw dropped, watching these two grown-ass men posturing like twelve-year-olds on a schoolyard, trading imaginary kung fu *Pokémon* moves—and I'm thinking, this movie is going to be mayhem... and it'll be a blast.

Big Big Brother

So here I am—injured, excited, and about to work with the legendary Sammo Hung. I mean, come on, Sammo! I was thrilled! But the second the crew found out I'd be doing fight scenes with him, they all gave me that look—you know the one. The "Oh no, girl, good luck with that" face.

Everyone kept saying, *"Sammo hits hard. Like, really hard. He's big, he's strong, and even the stunt guys don't like fighting him."* And I'm standing there with my busted knee thinking, "Great. This is gonna be fun."

We finally get to our first scene together. I had sorta, kinda told Sammo my leg was bothering me—but in classic Cynthia fashion, I was all, "No biggie! I can tough it out!" Meanwhile, inside I'm praying I don't have to do a backflip out the window and land on that leg.

The scene takes place in this hotel lobby—it's a fantastic fight sequence. It's also another one of my scenes where Sylvester Stallone showed his stunt team asking, *"How did she do that?!"*

This is the fight sequence where I do three rapid-fire kicks in the air—*bam, bam, BAM*—before landing. (I was wired for the take and it looked awesome!) Hong Kong wire teams are absolute geniuses with the fight choreography.

So anyway, Sammo's hitting me hard in the scene—and I mean *hard*—but I'm hanging in there, telling myself, Okay, not too bad. I've been through worse. Probably. Then the real chaos starts when I have to fight a group of stuntmen.

This takes me back to *Yes, Madam!*—on-set where a guy accidentally smacked me in the nose with a sword during a fight scene. This was the same kind of setup. I'm surrounded by guys, all swinging swords and fists, and I've got to do a spinning kick at one of them.

Problem is, this one stuntman keeps stepping way too close. I told him I'm kicking high multiple times. Is he listening? I stop and warn him again, "This is where my foot's going to be. Don't come any closer or you're going to get hit." Take number six, and nope—he steps into the wrong spot. I pulled my kick up high to avoid hitting him, and from up on the balcony, Sammo's yelling, "CUT! Too far! Too far! Close the gap!"

So I tell the guy again, nicely: "Seriously. Please stay back. I don't want to hit you."

Take seven—he steps in even closer. So again, I go over his head, and Sammo's now shouting like I just insulted his choreography. Now, I'm getting nervous. Sammo's getting mad. I'm sweating, and the pressure's building.

Finally, I again try to show the stuntman exactly where my foot will land. I do the kick slowly, foot extended, like "See? Right here. If you walk into this, that's on you."

We reset. Sammo yells, "Action!"

The guy comes in too close again.

BOOM! I spin—full speed—whack him right in the head… and he goes down hard.

He's practically unconscious on the floor, and I feel awful. I knew I was going to hit him. I told him I would hit him. But what am I supposed to do? It's only my second film! I'm trying to follow orders, trying not to get fired, and now I've just practically KO'd someone on set.

Then a crew member leans in and whispers, *"Sammo is grumpy today. He lost $300,000 gambling yesterday. That's why he's extra cranky."*

I'm thinking, *WHAT?! Well no wonder he's yelling like I stole his dim sum.*

Meanwhile, Sammo strolls over, claps, and goes, *"Great! Loved it! Move on!"* He's like nothing even happened. Doesn't check on the guy, doesn't blink.

I'm still standing there, basically on the verge of tears. Then one of the other stunt guys walks over and casually says, *"Hey, remember that guy who hit you in the nose with the sword in Yes, Madam!?"*

I say, *"Yeah..."*

He grins and points down at the guy, *"That's him."*

So I guess karma has a spinning back kick.

Horses, Sand and Fans

Now, one of the funniest scenes we shot—at least in theory—was the big horseback entrance. Richard Norton and I were supposed to ride in, flanked by what felt like three hundred stunt guys on horses. Epic, right?

Well... most of it ended up getting cut from the final film. But behind the scenes? Comedy gold.

So the day before the shoot, they tell us, "Okay, everyone, we're going to practice. These horses are all retired racehorses, so they're... a little spirited. We want you to get used to them."

That sounded reasonable enough.

We show up, and they assign horses. Richard gets this nice, manageable little horse. And me? They give me the biggest horse on the field. Like, absolutely massive. I look at the handler and go, "Seriously? Do you see how tall this horse is? I'm five foot-three on a good day!"

Before I can argue, they throw me on it. And the second I get in the saddle, the horse loses its mind. Bucking, rearing up—like it just found out it wasn't getting fed lunch. Meanwhile, I'm hanging on for dear life, wondering if anyone has a horse-sized parachute.

The handlers rush over—"Whoa whoa whoa! Too wild! Get her down!" And they pull me off. They tell me they'll get me another horse. So I wait… and wait… and wait. All day. Everyone else is out there trotting around, doing practice laps, having a grand old time. Me? Just standing there like a forgotten extra in a cowboy movie.

They finally say, "We'll get you a horse tomorrow for the real shoot."

Great. No practice. No idea what horse I'm riding. What could go wrong?

Next day, we're lined up for the big scene. Sammo strolls over and gives me this little gem of advice: "Cynthia… whatever you do, do not fall off. If you fall, a hundred horses are coming behind you. You'll get trampled."

Oh. That's super comforting.

So my new horse arrives, and thankfully, it's smaller. I breathe a little sigh of relief—until I try to line up with the rest of the group. My horse, apparently a bit of an introvert, refuses to get between the two bigger horses. Like, totally refuses. I'm nudging him, whispering sweet nothings, "Come on, buddy, don't embarrass me," and he starts kicking the horses next to him.

Now I've gone from "Wild Mustang of the Apocalypse" to "Timid Timmy with an Attitude." Great.

We eventually get into formation. Barely. I'm sitting next to Richard Norton, just trying not to fall off or die, and the camera starts to pan across the line of us—big dramatic moment. This is where we're all supposed to look serious and tough.

Sammo yells out, "Richard! Richard! Act! Act!"

Richard turns to me, completely confused, whispering, "What does he mean 'act'? I'm sitting on a horse, mate! Am I supposed to recite Macbeth up here?"

We both start giggling. I'm thinking, Yeah, let me just emote while sitting on a barely-trained horse who might throw me into a stampede.

Sammo then takes a stance in front of the group and yells, "All right, we're going to do a run-through." Now, whenever Sammo says "run-through," just know it means absolute chaos is about to happen, but we all smile, and nod like good little action stars.

He tells us the plan: "We're going to line up the horses and ride through this big sandstorm setup—super epic. We've got fifty giant industrial fans on one side, and fifty more on the other. Then, we're going to throw sand into the air while the fans are blasting. It'll look amazing, horses running through a giant dust cloud, very cinematic."

I'm thinking, "Industrial fans and a big pile of sand in front of them. Rambunctious race horses. What could possibly go wrong?"

And of course, before we start, Sammo gives us his favorite safety tip reminder: "Whatever you do—do not fall off your horse, or you get trampled… and die."

I'm now hearing "trampled and die" in surround sound rattling around in my brain.

Here's something you need to know about me: my eyes are super sensitive. Any bit of dust or bright light and I'm squinting like I've been staring into the sun for a week. So basically, if anything gets in my eyes—dirt, sand, even a suggestion of wind—it's game over.

So we mount up, and we start this big charge through the sandy battlefield. At first, I'm like, Okay, this isn't so bad, and then—SWOOSH! A sand paper laced dust devil was spinning right in my face.

Instant blindness.

My eyes slam shut, I'm bouncing around on this horse, and I'm trying to channel my inner Zen warrior thinking, "Stay on the horse, Cynthia. Don't fall, and die. Stay on the horse."

But it wasn't just me who was affected by the dust—the horses got sand in their eyes too. Now they're panicking, tossing their heads, veering all over the place like it's the Kentucky Derby meets a natural disaster movie.

We come out the other end of the "run-through" and, no joke, everyone is scattered. The whole formation is gone. People are riding sideways, backward, and diagonally. One guy somehow ended up behind the fans. And sure enough, a stunt guy actually did fall off his horse, and got trampled. Everyone's stumbling around, coughing up sand, trying to blink again. I'm halfway convinced I'll never see clearly again.

Sammo walks in, and yells, "Yeah… that's not gonna work."

So, after that chaos, Sammo decides maybe a hundred fans, and a biblical-level sandstorm are a bit much. He scales it back to about five fans—just enough to give a little heroic dust poof without blinding the cast and triggering a horse mutiny.

And we reshoot the scene over and over—all day long. It took thirteen hours of charging, rearing, shouting, and a ton of sand. By the end of it, I had dust in places I didn't even know existed. And when you finally watch the scene in the movie? It's like... ten seconds of cinematic glory. Ten glorious dust-filled seconds.

Sweating Like a Boss

Sammo wanted this movie to be a huge ensemble—tons of stars, lots of action, comedy, martial arts—because it was going to be released for Chinese New Year.

Now, if you don't know, Chinese New Year is basically the *Super Bowl* of movie releases in Hong Kong. Every director pulls out the big guns. It's like a cinematic arms race—who can have the biggest explosions, wildest fights, and most famous cameos. And there I was, on my second movie ever, still trying to figure out where craft services was.

I did, however, learn one thing from *Yes, Madam!*: how to pad up. That was my new specialty—sneaking pads into my costume. I was becoming a human piñata. You hit me? You're hitting a bit of foam too. Lesson #1 in survival.

So Sammo comes over and says, "Okay, Cynthia, you and Richard—you are cavalry soldiers from America."

I'm like, "Oh, cool. Like Western-style?"

"No… Confederate soldiers."

I gave Richard the look and we both kind of shrugged. Richard says, "Sure thing. We're American Confederates now."

Don't ask questions—just ride the horse, and wear a crazy outfit.

So then comes the costume fitting. Sammo tells us, "Your scene is set in winter." Okay, but we are filming in Hong Kong—in mid-July. Now, for context: July in Hong Kong is like a hot yoga class with humidity that slaps you in the face every time you breathe. And Sammo tells me, "You'll wear three shirts, two pairs of pants."

I blinked. "Three shirts? Two pants?"

"It's winter," he says, very seriously.

So I gear up. And let me tell you—these weren't breezy cotton t-shirts. We're talking full-on wool, thick, historical-military-grade clothing. I felt like I was wrapped in a weighted blanket, inside a sauna, wearing a fireplace.

I turned to Richard and said, "I feel like a sweaty marshmallow in a Civil War uniform." And he wasn't doing much better—he was pouring sweat. Niagara Falls of sweat.

And the best part? They didn't have backup costumes. So when we were done with a take, they'd take a with a 1982 Conair hairdryer—and start blasting Richard's armpits. That's some wardrobe magic, right there—let's smoke the room with *eau de armpit*. The wool was drenched with sweat. That means we had the pleasure of repeatedly wearing our hot, damp, sweat-soaked clothes before every take. Yuck!

Neither Richard nor I realized until after sweating buckets in triple layers that—wait a minute—we didn't need to wear anything underneath—only what would be on camera. I should have gone full commando under the uniform—it might have been almost breathable.

There's no black belt in "how not to die of heat stroke in a wool uniform in sweltering Hong Kong summer heat." But hey—I survived, learned a lot, and the movie turned out great. Even if we looked like melting Civil War reenactors doing spinning kicks.

Big Budget, No Time, and a Little Luck

Sammo built an entire town for *Millionaires Express*. A full-on Western-style set, complete with a hotel, saloon, streets, the works. He wasn't messing around. But here's the thing: he was stressed. Like, next-level Hong Kong film industry stress. And with good reason.

Most Hong Kong action films back then took forever to shoot. I'm talking five and a half months, sometimes eight months if things got crazy. But this film? Sammo only had a month. One month to shoot a huge action-comedy period piece with 300 stunt people and a town full of explosions and horse chases. Madness!

So what did Sammo do? He basically locked us in.

Okay, not literally—but almost. He didn't want anyone leaving the set between shoots to cut down the shoot schedule between takes. The crew built this faux hotel on set that looked great on camera but also doubled as housing. There were beds, cots, random sofas—you name it. It was like a cinematic sleepover... except no one was having fun, and everyone smelled like horses and week-old sweat.

I was so exhausted one night, I laid down, eyes closed, trying to sneak in five minutes of sleep. And this little wardrobe lady walks up and pokes me in the face. Not even gently—a hard poke, right under the eye. I groan and open one lid, and she says, "Don't close your eyes! If you sleep, you'll get bags under your eyes!"

I blinked at her like, "Ma'am… I do not care. I'll look like a zombie in this scene—I just need sleep." But nope. No rest for the weary when you're making a Sammo Hung Chinese New Year epic.

We would sometimes shoot for two and a half days straight. I wish I were exaggerating. Then finally, someone would say, "Okay, you can go home now—to shower."

A shower! What a luxury! Except—plot twist—there were no showers. None. And did I mention the 300 stunt people?

How about bathrooms? Also none. No porta-potties. No trailers. No discreet little outhouses. Just… empty shell buildings in the background. Someone would just gesture and say, "See those buildings over there? Just… go in there."

These structures weren't finished off. They were props. Dirt floors, no walls, no plumbing, and... let's just say you'd better watch where you stepped or you'd be slipping around like you were in a kung fu version of *Wipeout*. But you know what? According to the Chinese crew, stepping in… shit… was actually good luck. "No worry, Cynthia!" they'd say. "Very lucky! You step in, good fortune!"

I nearly broke my neck trying to avoid someone else's "good luck." Although I'll take their word for it, but I was still burning my shoes afterward.

Despite all that—sweat, sand, stampedes, and stepping in questionable substances—Richard and I pulled it off. We made it through that wild, dusty, sweaty month and came out with a film that, honestly, is a classic.

Even though my ACL never really fully healed—it disintegrated. I learned how to work around it and just tape it, brace it, ignore it. You just push through. That's the Hong Kong way. You fall down, you get up. You're bleeding? Keep rolling. You step in something weird? Hey, good luck!

Millionaires Express was among one of the toughest, craziest, most exhausting films I ever made—but also one of the most memorable.

CHAPTER 5

MAGIC CRYSTAL

"Fear is just a signal that you're about to do something powerful. Don't back down—breathe, face it head-on, and let that angst fuel your strength. That's where real courage begins."

Magic Crystal was directed by Wong Jing, which already tells you we were going to be mixing wild action with a healthy dose of pandemonium. I was really excited to do this one, though, because unlike most of my previous Hong Kong films, this one had a bit of a jet-setting vibe. We were filming in not one, not two, but three exotic locations: Hong Kong, Greece, and Taiwan. This felt like a big-budget Bond film, or at least the martial arts version of one.

Right around that time in the '80s, there had been a bombing in Libya and some atmospheric radiation scare floating around the news. Not the most relaxing time for traveling Americans. So we're prepping to go to Greece, and the local crew's saying, "Oh, it's fine, we're Chinese. Terrorists won't bother us."

I look around and say, “Wait a minute. You’re all Chinese. I’m not.”

They look at me, smile, and go, “Just wear a Canadian flag on your jacket. You'll be fine.”

Oh sure. Problem solved. Instant camouflage: courtesy of Canada.

Luckily, everything was fine. No drama, no diplomatic incidents, and I even got to work with Richard Norton on that shoot. When you’re flying off to foreign countries where the film permit situation is a little... shall we say uncertain, it’s comforting to have someone you know on set with you.

So, we start filming in Hong Kong like usual—but then, off we go to Greece. And I was so excited. I thought, “Finally! Greece! I’ve never been!”

I had ten full days there. I'm thinking of all the sightseeing I’m going to do. Now, guess how many days I worked? All ten. Every single day. Nonstop.

Meanwhile, Richard only had one day of filming in Greece. The producers felt it was easier logistically to just keep him there for the whole shoot. So he and his wife Judy were out sightseeing every day—eating baklava, taking boat rides, living their best Grecian lives.

I, on the other hand, was doing a grueling schedule sweating under bright lights, dodging punches, and trying to pretend I wasn’t dying of jet lag.

I did get to see the Parthenon... during my lunch break. I skipped food and ran over in costume just to peek at the Acropolis. That counts as sightseeing, right?

Now, technically, you're not allowed to film action scenes—or have weapons—anywhere near those ancient sites. But this was a Hong Kong film. Which means... well, let's just say the rules were more like suggestions.

The producers had someone stationed to act as a lookout. If no one was around, they'd sneak in the prop guns and go, "Quick, quick! Action!" We were literally filming fight scenes on the fly, ducking behind ruins when tourists came by. "Hide the sword! Hide the gun!" It was guerrilla filmmaking at its finest. Pretty sure we were filming illegally, but it looked great on screen.

Scared for Life

Richard, Sharla Cheung, and I were filming an intense sword fight scene, and we'd been going at it for something like 24 hours straight. That's not even exaggerating. Sleep-deprived, a little wobbly, and trying to remember the choreography, I went in for a sword strike… Richard missed his cue and didn't duck… wham—right to his forehead.

Instant scar above his eye.

They shuttle him off to the hospital stitched him up, threw in a double while he was being sewn back together (basically a stuntman, Richard's sweaty wardrobe and a blonde wig), and then—because he's a total pro—Richard came back to the set and finished the fight scene with the stitches in. The scar was permanent. And believe me, he reminded me every time we saw each other from that day forward.

"Hey Cynthia, remember that time you scalped me in Greece?"

"Yes, Richard. I remember."

That wasn't the only mishap. *Magic Crystal* was also the first film where I got to use a spear. Now, weapons are kind of my thing—I've trained in all sorts of traditional Chinese weapons: hook swords, sabers, double broadswords… you name it. So when they said I'd be doing staff work, I asked if I could upgrade to the spear and show some of my own moves.

They loved the idea. Not many people were showing spear work in films back then, so it was a cool showcase. The only problem was my knee.

I tore my ACL before filming *Millionaires Express*, and it never really fully healed. It'd go from "fine" to "totally gone" without warning. So right in the middle of filming this big fight scene in a public square in Greece, my knee gives out again.

Just snaps. I can barely walk.

But of course, being Hong Kong cinema, they're like, "Can you keep going?"

So I do. I'm fighting with a spear, practically limping in circles, trying not to fall over.

At one point, I go to jab a guy in the stomach—and because I'm off-balance—*schwing*.

Right to his groin.

Cut! Cut! Cut!

Poor guy dropped like a sack of bricks, and I was mortified.

Thankfully I pulled back a bit, so it didn't do any permanent damage. But I've never forgotten the look on his face. That was real.

Honestly, that shot was so intense I kind of wish they had kept it in. Definitely great for a blooper reel… just with more pain.

Sweating in the Eighties

Greece is hot. No air conditioning. Wardrobe was a one-costume-only kind of situation. They gave Richard Norton this brown outfit, and he was sweating like crazy—huge sweat patches under his arms. So between takes, wardrobe would come in with a hair dryer, lift his arm, and start blow-drying him like a roast chicken. I was dying laughing. It's hard to act tough when someone's baking your armpits.

And guess what? I only had one costume too. They actually came up to me and said, "Hey Cynthia, can we borrow your pants for the stunt guy?"

I said, "Absolutely not. He's been sweating, rolling on the ground, and now you want me to wear them afterward? Nope. Find another black pair." Sometimes you gotta draw the line at shared pants.

Kung Fu Mash-up

Now, let's talk about that final fight scene—honestly, one of my favorites from the film. They had me doing Praying Mantis, which wasn't a style I had trained in before. So they had to teach me the choreography on the spot—which is very Hong Kong-style, by the way:

"Here's a new martial art. Learn it by lunch." But it was fun. Praying Mantis is tricky—it's all finger traps and lightning-fast strikes.

At one point in the scene, I had to hit Richard in his temple with a thumb strike.

He looks at me and says, "Cynthia, your thumb isn't gonna knock me out."

And I'm like, "Oh, come on, give the thumb some respect."

So yep, we have the infamous thumb to the temple strike captured on film. Who needs fists when you've got a bionic thumb?

I also snuck in some Eagle Claw, which was my addition. I'd gone to China to study the eagle form, and it's beautiful—it mimics how an eagle strikes, with sweeping feather-like movements. I loved mixing it into the choreography. You don't get to see a lot of traditional styles like that in action films, so that was a real treat. Fans definitely picked up on it too—lots of questions later about the forms I used. So yes, eagle + mantis = kung fu mash-up magic.

Now… how did we collaborate on those fight scenes? Well, Richard had a bit of a struggle. He's hardcore Okinawan karate—very strong, very direct. Not exactly the flowy Chinese style. So when the choreographer had him doing kung fu, he was like, "I don't know what to do with my hands!"

If you watch the scene, you'll see him kind of do this awkward flower-hand thing before going into tiger claw. He hated it. But honestly, he pulled it off. It took a while, but looked great on screen. I always teased him about that flower-hand moment.

E.T.—No Phone Home

Let's not forget the makeshift alien. That *thing* was... well, let's call it creative design. It looked like a green paper-mâché blob with duct tape holding it together. And it was supposed to be *Venus*—the most beautiful woman in the universe!

Richard and I would just crack up on set. And in the spaceship scene, we finally see the full alien. It's talking, but its lips aren't moving. So it's just this unmoving mouth, and a dubbed voice going, "Greetings, Earthlings."

The funny part is, we had no idea what we were reacting to when we filmed it. I remember Wong Jing saying, "Okay Cynthia, for this shot come in here and look up at the ceiling."

I asked, "Why?"

He says, "Don't worry. Just look up."

So I'm staring up like I'm admiring the paint job.

Turns out, in the movie, I'm supposed to be reacting to an alien invasion. Would've been nice to know! I could've at least added some "Oh no, aliens!" facial expression. But no—just me and my neutral ceiling gaze.

Still, with editing, the scene looked fine.

Speaking of "magic," the story was definitely a little inspired by the film *E.T.* There was this glowing crystal, some government bad guys… total Hong Kong-style sci-fi adventure.

They were always doing those unofficial remakes. Like *Prince of the Sun,* that was their *Golden Child* clone. And I saw one film that literally had the *Jaws* theme playing in the background—just, straight up stole it. Hello… can you say copyright infringement?

One of the scenes I actually loved shooting was on a speedboat. I'm a total water person, so being on that boat, flying across the ocean, was my idea of fun. That was the one moment where I felt like I was on vacation.

And finally, how'd the movie do in Hong Kong? Surprisingly well! I mean, it was cheesy. No doubt about it. But sometimes, the cornier it is, the more people love it. And this one had all the ingredients: aliens, kung fu, glowing crystals, and Richard Norton getting blow-dried between takes. What more could you want?

Magic Crystal was one of those "glamorous" international films where you end up sunburned, sleep-deprived, and possibly armed without a permit. But it was also fun.

CHAPTER 6

RIGHTING WRONGS
(AKA ABOVE THE LAW)

"Setbacks aren't the end—they're just God's way of pointing you toward a new path. Every stumble is an opportunity in disguise, a chance to rise stronger, smarter, and more unstoppable than before."

Righting Wrongs, or as some people know it, *Above the Law*—which, by the way, has absolutely nothing to do with the Steven Seagal movie of the same name. A totally different film. Less ponytail with more kicking.

This was technically my third Hong Kong film. First *Yes, Madam*, then *Millionaires Express*, and then came this gem. Here's the twist: I was supposed to be the antagonist in Jackie Chan's *Armour of God*. I was over the moon. Jackie is my idol! When I was younger and training in kung fu, I'd go watch his movies in Chinatown theaters, then run home and try to copy everything I saw on screen *(usually without breaking too many lamps)*. I was finally going to work with him. My dream come true!

But then Jackie had a terrible fall from the tree, ended up needing surgery, and the production halts. I was crushed. *Golden Harvest* calls and says, "Well, we've got another film for you: *Righting Wrongs*, with Yuen Biao." I was disappointed at first, but then I thought, hey, another movie, more butt-kicking, let's go!

Before I headed back to Hong Kong, I was at my martial arts school in Northern California doing jumping hook kicks like a maniac because I wanted to be in top form. And it happens again—crack—my knee goes out. I'd blown out my anterior cruciate ligament. My doctor basically said, "Yeah, you're not kicking anything for a while." I said, "I've got five days before I leave for Hong Kong!" His response? "Good luck with that."

So I show up on the set for film *Righting Wrongs* with a busted right leg—which, of course, is my dominant kicking leg. Every kick I throw in that film? It's my left leg. Watching it now, I think, "Wow, that looked okay!" But filming it? I felt like a baby giraffe learning to walk.

Working with Yuen Biao—what a gift. Out of everyone I've ever fought on screen, he's my favorite. Our timing was spot-on, and we just clicked. There's this one fight scene in a house, and Yuen Biao does this insane stunt: he flips and lands on a rocking chair, balancing on the arms, and just stares at me like, "Yeah, I did that." No wires. No CGI. Just pure, gravity-defying kung fu magic. I think it took him about twenty tries, but when he nailed it, I was in awe.

Steel Whip Anyone?

Corey Yuen says, "We need a female villain who's good with a steel whip. Know anyone?" I say, "Sure—Karen Sheperd can do that." They bring her out, but she's got a couple of script concerns: one, she didn't want to be killed by me because it might hurt her image; and two, she plays an evil character who kills a child in the film and she wanted no part of that.

So Corey cheats these scenes. When they filmed the segment where her character was supposed to be killed off by me, they filmed her running away from me instead. All good and she leaves the set. Then after she's clear from the shoot location, a stuntman puts on a wig and her outfit, and I'm filmed killing him. Oh, and that scene where her character snuffs the child? That was an insert shot added later during post production. They again used a stuntman with a tight shot of her character's hands stabbing a boy. I'm sure it was quite a surprise to Karen when she saw the final edit.

The staff vs. whip fight between Karen and me—that was hands-down one of the most beautifully choreographed fight scenes I've done. We were up on scaffolding, whipping and spinning around. Let me tell you, getting hit with a steel whip is not fun. That thing has a mind of its own. You're going home bruised no matter what. I even had one moment where I was in a full split, hanging from wires, and they dropped me onto her. It looked cool, but ouch.

Yuen Biao got hurt too. There's a scene where he jumps off a balcony—no stunt double, no wires, just him and a mattress hidden under some grass. He stuck the landing like a champ, but his back paid the price. That guy was fearless.

Now here's the real kicker: in the original ending, both of our characters die. I get a drill bit through my throat (super dramatic), and Yuen Biao falls out of a plane. Roll credits.

When that version screened in Hong Kong the audience absolutely loses it. Booing, yelling, throwing stuff at the screen, screaming—"No! Don't kill her! Don't kill her!" At that time I'm back in the States filming *China O'Brien*, and *Golden Harvest* calls me: "You have to come back. We need to reshoot the ending. You're alive now." I said, "Uh... my hair's totally different. I'm in the middle of another movie!" They say, "It's fine, no one will notice."

So back I go. They shoot a new ending where I only get stabbed in the arm, and Yuen Biao survives by landing in water. I save him with a boat. Everyone's happy. Big hit. Moral of the story: don't kill your heroes. Especially if they're me.

There are two versions of this film floating around—one where Cynthia dies, and one where Cynthia lives. So if you're a collector, go hunting!

My Biggest Fan

My mom was so excited to see something from my new film. She's my biggest fan on the planet. I sent her a photo of me with a stake through my throat, blood everywhere, thinking she'd get a kick out of the behind-the-scenes makeup. What does she do? She gives the pic to the *Scranton Times*. They run the picture in the local paper. I was like, "Mom! Really? *That picture?!*"

Righting Wrongs (or *Above the Law*—pick your title) took about five and a half months to shoot. It was grueling. I think they liked me because no matter how banged up I got, I'd show up the next day ready to go. Crazy? Maybe. Passionate? Definitely.

Of all the action scenes I've done, *Righting Wrongs* has some of my absolute favorites. So if you haven't seen it yet, check it out—both endings if you can.

Cynthia lives! (Or doesn't… depends on the cut.)

CHAPTER 7

NO RETREAT, NO SURRENDER 2

"Fear is just a signal that you're about to do something powerful. Don't back down—breathe, face it head-on, and let that angst fuel your strength. That's where real courage begins."

No Retreat, No Surrender 2 was supposed to be my first movie ever. That was the plan. Yuen Kwai (a.k.a. Corey Yuen) flew out to L.A., and auditioned people for the "next Bruce Lee". He saw me, liked what he saw, signed me, and I was supposed to do this film with *Seasonal Films*. Well… nothing happened for a year and a half. I thought, "Oh well… maybe he changed his mind." Welcome to showbiz!

World News Tonight

I keep doing my thing, and I get on the cover of a martial arts magazine, and—out of nowhere—Peter Jennings' *World News Tonight* calls. Apparently, someone on his team saw my cover and thought, "We need to put her on the news." So they did a five-minute segment on me, and I said something like, "I'm supposed to be doing a movie in Hong Kong with Corey Yuen, but no one's called me yet." The segment ends with me dramatically wielding a sword, and them saying, *"Look out, Hong Kong—here she comes!"*

Well… Sammo Hung is watching *World News Tonight* —in Hong Kong—and asks, "Who's that?" Calls up Corey Yuen and says, "I want to use her in *Yes Madam*." Corey says, "That's the girl I already picked!" So, bam, I get a call, I'm on a plane, and suddenly I'm shooting *Yes Madam*. And it became a massive hit!

So now, *Seasonal Films* is like, "Hey! Wait a minute! We have a contract with her!" So off I go to do *No Retreat, No Surrender 2*. Not the first movie I filmed, but technically the second one released—and my first English-speaking role, which, as you'll see, didn't necessarily make things easier.

Doppelgängers?

I hadn't yet seen the first *No Retreat, No Surrender,* but I knew Jean-Claude Van Damme and Kurt McKinney were in it. So I fly to Thailand, ready to work with Jean-Claude and Kurt. Corey Yuen meets me and says, "Okay, Cynthia, this is the guy you're co-staring with in the movie." I look over and… huh?

Let's just say... the guy looked nothing like Kurt McKinney.

I was standing there thinking, "Am I being Punk'd? Is this some weird kung fu doppelgänger prank?" Turns out, Jean-Claude bailed to go do *Bloodsport*—good career move for him—and word is, he convinced Kurt to bail, too—told him shooting in Thailand was too dangerous. *(Not totally untrue—just ask my knee.)*

So now they're scrambling. They pick up the phone looking to fill the McKinney and Van Damme roles, and called a karate school in the Los Angeles area— Loren Avedon happened to pick up.

Producer: "We're looking for someone who can fight and be in Thailand tomorrow."

Loren Avedon: "You're talking to him!"

Producer: "Great. You're hired."

And just like that—Lauren is suddenly in the film with a lead role. Matthias Hues was brought in to fill the Jean-Claude role. Big guy with blonde hair who looked like a Viking on protein powder—close enough.

And then the craziness began.

Muay Thai Madness

We're filming in Thailand—in 1986—which is already its own adventure. The first fight scene I do is in a real Muay Thai gym. And the guys there are not happy. "No women in the ring," they tell us. "Girls don't belong in the ring." I thought, "Seriously? What century are we in?"

So I fought outside the ring. Then they saw me fight and said, "Okay, maybe she can fight in the ring... but she can't enter like a man." That's why in the film, you'll see me rolling under the ropes to get in. Not a style choice. Just the only way they'd allow me in.

Trains, Pains and Brains

Then there was this scene we shot on railroad tracks—way out in Kanchanaburi. Middle of nowhere. The "hotel" had no air conditioning and a bowling alley for entertainment. So we bowled every night for two months. It was bowling or lose our minds.

Getting to the tracks was sketchy. You had to hike a mile down with all the equipment. I remember the director saying, "Okay, if a train comes, find a spot to jump off the tracks. There won't be time to outrun it." Oh, great. We're doing live train stunts with no exit strategy. One crew member even had his ear to the rail listening for vibrations. Like a cowboy movie.

Meanwhile, I'm trying to deliver this line about a "bowl of veggies," and I kept butchering it because I was sweating, exhausted, and nervous about being hit by a train.

Then comes the bug scene. One night, they bring me a bucket—I'm not kidding—full of venomous bugs. The idea is: they'll put one on my chest, and it'll crawl up my neck for a dramatic scene. I'm like, "WHAT?!" They say, "Don't worry, we'll take the poison out." I said, "How? Sit it down for a little detox therapy?" Of course, the bug wouldn't perform. Wouldn't crawl when they said "Action!" So what do they do? They sew a live bug to my shirt. I am not okay with this. It had like a hundred legs, and it was doing this weird squirmy dance all over me. I still have nightmares.

Max Thayer was a lot of fun on-set—amazing actor, great guy. He had this scene where he had to drink fresh snake blood. Yes, that's a thing. To get him to do it, they told him it helps with male virility "It will put lead in your pencil" (um… snake viagra?), so he agreed to do it, but only if we did the scene in one take. So they cut a real snake, pour the blood, and he chugs it like it's a protein shake. He said it tasted like warm, salty soup. I was just glad I didn't have to drink it too.

Oh—and the monkey brains? That wasn't a Hollywood prop. It was also real. Thank God I wasn't in that scene. I would've cried. I still gag thinking about it.

Wong Jung-Lee was in the film too, and he kicked hard. They gave me a little pad for protection during one scene, and of course, he managed to hit everywhere except the pad. Thanks, Wong.

I also had to do a stunt where Matthias kicks me into a wall, and I get yanked back with a wire and a mini explosion. First time I ever had explosives strapped to my chest. I was praying harder than a nun in a lightning storm.

Speaking of Matthias—he wasn't a trained martial artist back then. He was an actor trying to survive this mayhem. There's a scene where he gets dragged along the ground, and since they couldn't find a stunt double that looked like him (hello, six foot-five blonde beast), he had to do the stunt himself. He messed up his back from that stunt—and honestly, I think it still bothers him today.

We all had our moments, though. I warned the guys not to do the weird dubbing faces—like that classic Hong Kong, "Who? Me?" gesture pointing your finger to your nose. Guess who did it anyway? Matthias. We were like, "Noooo!" And if you watch the movie closely, someone still dubbed me going "Huh?" with my eyes wide open. It wasn't me! I swear!

Ants and Elephants

There was a scene that ultimately ended up on the cutting-room floor in which Loren Avedon and I were riding an elephant—he in front, me behind him. Neither of us had any idea how to control the animal, so the producers brought in a handler. Unfortunately, the handler was caught on camera, creating continuity issues, and that alone was enough to kill the scene.

But there were two additional problems. First, the elephant was covered in red fire ants, which were biting us relentlessly. You try to stay professional and act like nothing's wrong, but we were both wriggling on the elephant as hundreds of crimson bugs nipped at our skin. Second, Loren's long legs draped naturally over the elephant's sides, while my much shorter legs were stretched into a full split, dangling awkwardly on either side. I'm not sure that qualified as cinematic excellence.

Later, the producers asked if we wanted to ride the elephant back to base instead of walking. Since it was a long hike, we happily said yes—right up until we realized there was no handler. Before we could say we'd changed our minds, and walk back instead, the elephant took off like the lead bull in a stampede. We clung on for dear life, convinced this was how we were going out, only to discover later that the elephant wasn't panicking at all—he was just sprinting back to base for his water break.

Hands Off, Buddy

My character also had to die in this movie. They put explosives on me when I get riddled with machine gun rounds, and Max—ever the method actor—starts sobbing over my lifeless body (real tears)… and during the emotional moment he full-on grabs my chest when he cradles me. I was thinking, "Max! I know I'm playing dead, but I'm not a play thing. What are you doing?!" He swore he didn't realize he was grabbing me inappropriately, he just got lost in the moment. I said, "Next time, lose yourself somewhere else, buddy—not on my boobs."

For the helicopter scene they flew us in these rickety old military choppers that looked like they belonged in a museum or a helicopter boneyard. These deathtraps coughed, sputtered, made terrible noises, but hey—we lived!

Funny story—years later, Brian Doyle-Murray (Bill Murray's brother, and a friend of mine) calls me at 2am and says, "Were you a helicopter pilot in Cambodia? I just saw you in a movie piloting a heli!" Yep. That was me.

Last crazy moment—there's a scene where we had to jump into a river after an explosion. The water looked like pea green soup. Disgusting. We figured it was algae… until we saw elephants and buffalo peeing in it after we jumped in. That's right, not pea soup, it was pee pee soup. Great! Now I'm swimming in an animal toilet. The producers even tried to color-correct the water in post—thought it was a camera color issue. Nope. Didn't work either. It stayed pea-green in the final edit.

All in all? Total madness. But somehow, we finished the movie. And despite the bugs, explosions, animal pee, train danger, and accidental fondling—I think it turned out pretty good. Well… except for the poster. I don't know what they did to my face on that thing. But hey, *No Retreat, No Surrender 2*—it lived up to its name.

CHAPTER 8

INSPECTORS WEAR SKIRTS

"When you show up—fully, boldly, and ready—doors start to open that you never even knew existed. Opportunity doesn't always knock; sometimes it waits to see if you're brave enough to walk up and turn the handle (or side kick the door in)."

Inspectors Wear Skirts is not a film that most people usually list when rattling off my Hong Kong classics—but let me tell you, it's got some killer fight scenes. Hard core fans ask me about it all the time, like it's this hidden martial arts Easter egg. Which, in a way, it kind of is.

So here's how it all came together: I was actually smack in the middle of shooting *Blonde Fury* when Jackie Chan was producing this movie. A super innovative concept at the time: all women leads, throwing down with style. Love that. But halfway through filming, *Golden Harvest* apparently looked at the footage and remarked, "Hmm, you know what this needs? Some Cynthia Rothrock."

So they borrowed me for a week—literally yanked me off the *Blonde Fury* set like I was on loan from a martial arts library—and wrote me into the movie. A brand new character, brand new fight scenes, no big deal, just jump in mid-plot and start kicking some booty.

Honestly, they did a pretty good job stitching me into the story. You'd almost never guess I wasn't in the script from day one. The teams are highly creative and always made the scenes work.

One of my favorite parts was working with Jeff Falcon. Jeff's great—he and I both trained in Chinese Wushu, so we spoke the same martial arts language. Except he's fluent in Monkey, and I'm fluent in Eagle. There's a scene where we're literally doing Monkey Style vs. Eagle Style. I mean, if someone told me I'd be fighting a man pretending to be a monkey on camera, I would've asked what kind of movie this was. What they captured was creative and something fresh. Monkey hand flicks versus Eagle claws—pure kung fu fun.

Weapons-wise, I got to use a cane, which I loved. It's like the grandpa of all weapons—practical, stylish, and totally capable of taking someone's kneecaps out. I got to combine it with a broadsword and a tonfa, because why not toss several of my favorite martial arts weapons into a fight?

One of the most ridiculous, and brilliant fight scenes: I drop-kick a grenade back at a ninja. Eventually, I pull the ninja up a flagpole—and then he explodes. Because... logic. The stunt choreography team went all out. Table flips, grenades, flaming flagpoles. This was classic '80s Hong Kong cinema. Subtlety was definitely left at the door.

There was a sequence where I light a track drenched in kerosene on fire and just stand there... with my face next to the flames for the dramatic camera shot. I said, "Hey, maybe we should test this without me first." You know, see how it goes. *(I may be fearless, but I'm not flame proof.)*

Good thing I spoke up, because the stunt guy who tested it got his eyebrows singed off. I said, "Yeah, I think I'll be staying back from the kerosene." Thanks to my friend Mang Hoi who once told me, "Cynthia, you need to look out for yourself. No one else is going to." Best advice ever. Saved my face—and my brows.

The movie was produced by *Golden Harvest*, and I have so many great memories from those days. I grew up watching their films with my Sifu, Shum Leung, in New York. We'd train Eagle Claw and then hit the Chinatown theater to watch the latest kung fu flick. Getting to be in one of those movies was surreal. Although Jackie Chan wasn't on set while I was filming, it was a great opportunity to be in one of his films.

Nowadays, people watch these movies and ask, "Did you actually do all your fights and stunts?" And I just smile. No CGI. No digital doubles. That was me, flipping, kicking, and almost catching on fire .

If you've never seen *Inspectors Wear Skirts*, go check it out. This flick has it all: strong women, fantastic fight scenes, ridiculous ninja explosions—and yes, plenty of monkey-versus-eagle action.

One of my favorite moments is when a bad guy tosses a hand grenade at my character, and I casually kick it right back at him. Not exactly practical, but it's classic Hong Kong action style.

What more could you want?

CHAPTER 9

LADY REPORTER
(AKA BLONDE FURY)

"If I was born with nine lives— I once nearly used them all on one film set! But that's the beauty of this journey: every close call, every wild stunt, every 'how did I survive that?' moment reminds me that living fully means daring boldly."

The Lady Reporter also known as *Blonde Fury* is by far one of the hardest films I've done. And by *hardest*, I mean I genuinely thought I wasn't going to make it off the set alive.

Let's take a little walk through the chaos, scene by scene.

Baby, Cardboard, and a Minor Nose Realignment

The movie kicks off with me arriving as a journalist investigating low-income housing. You know, your average martial arts heroine moment. Then—boom—there's a fire. Naturally, I rush in to save a baby.

Now, here's where the fun begins. Director Mang Hoi looks at me and casually goes, "Cynthia, can you jump off that building?" It's two stories. And I'm like, "Sure, I guess I can?" Because when you're standing on the ground looking up, it feels doable. Then I climb up there and look down, and suddenly I'm five-foot-three plus two floors of nope.

He tells me not to worry—I'll be landing on "safety equipment." Which turned out to be a pile of... cardboard boxes and an old mattress. That's it. No airbags. Not even a trampoline from someone's garage sale. Oh, and he adds, "We'll set off an explosion behind you. So when I say action, you must jump. Otherwise, the flames will engulf you, and you will get bad burns."

So there I am, holding a fake baby (which means no arms for balance), wearing heels (because journalism, apparently), and waiting for my cue two stories up. I barely here *Action!* and I feel intense heat behind me. The adrenaline kicks in and I leap—heels first—like some kind of martial arts Mary Poppins, narrowly avoiding a fireball that would've turned me into crispy Cynthia. I crash-land into some cardboard boxes and the paper-thin mattress, only for my knees to ricochet into my nose like a heat-seeking missile. I genuinely thought I'd broken my nose.

But before I could even finish wondering how bad my nose was, Mang Hoi strolled over and said, "There was a problem with the shot. We need you to do it again."

So I did it again. Then a few more high-impact, bone-rattling stunts for good measure.

After that, with my legs sore as heck, they had me do about twenty takes holding a fake baby, jumping from roughly ten feet and sticking the landing like a gymnast in heels.

After a while, I wasn't feeling so hot—shocking, I know—so they carted me off to see a traditional Chinese doctor.

The doctor examined me, frowned with grave concern, and said, "Your internal organs are all jumbled up."

Which, frankly, sounded about right.

Then the doc handed me a small pouch of mysterious pills and cheerfully added, "Take these, and you'll be fine in the morning."

Of course I will. Because nothing says "movie magic" like a bruised nose, jumbled organs, and a second chance at spontaneous combustion.

Basket of Doom

Later, they brought me back for reshoots. New director, new hair style *(spoiler: it changes a lot during this flick)*, and a new death-defying stunt. I'm on a scaffold, four floors up, and they want me to jump into a wicker basket being held up by two stuntmen with a rope.

That was the safety equipment—my life in the hands of two guys with no harness.

And this basket? It doesn't have a bottom. Just an open hole in the center. I had to sit like a human wishbone with my legs splayed over the edges to avoid falling through it. I kept begging the stunt guys, "Please don't let go of the rope, okay? Stay focused."

The Power of Toilet Paper

There's a fight scene in the movie where I'm throwing down with martial artist Vincent Lyn. We're battling it out inside a bunch of shipping crates—tight quarters, full-force strikes, nowhere to hide.

One part of our fight choreography included a groin kick. Right in the jewels.

Before we filmed the scene I asked Vincent, "Hey, you've got a protective cup on, right?"

Vincent, cool as ever, goes, "Uhhh... no."

I just blinked at him like, What do you mean no!?

He says, "They didn't have a cup. They just gave me a roll of toilet paper and I stuffed my drawers with it... that's all they could find."

Vincent basically turned his crotch into a Charmin fortress, and hoped for the best.

So we go to shoot the scene, and I deliver the kick with precision, as Mang Hoi wanted full contact. Bam! Nailed 'em. I look at Vincent's face and—oh, that pained expression. That wasn't acting. That was 100% real-life bean-bag ouchy.

In true professional fashion, Vincent finished the scene like a champ—even though I'm pretty sure he needed an ice pack and a moment of silence afterward.

I still laugh when I rewatch that scene. Every time I see his face scrunch up, I think, That is not a method acting, that's toilet paper fail.

Ropes, Rope Burns, and Really Bad News

Then comes the infamous rope fight scene. Giant crane, probably 150 feet high, me dangling from ropes like a *Cirque du Soleil* dropout. I had no idea ropes could burn so bad. Every time I bounced off one, I lost a layer of skin.

I was wired up, sure—but one poor stuntman broke his leg, and another got paralyzed when the rope rig collapsed. That shook me. It reminded me just how insane and dangerous these Hong Kong stunts could be. There was no padding and definitely no OSHA safety standards or requirements. This was as sketchy as safety is, packed with pure adrenaline, and your last will and testament.

Ratatoo-eek!

And just when you thought this movie couldn't get any more outrageous… let's talk about the rat.

There's a hilarious fight scene in the film where a minion (Chung Fat) is sent to steal an incriminating file from character Judy Yu's house that ends with him getting a large rat stuck in his mouth.

And here's the crazy part: it wasn't a fake rat. It was a live one—a scurrying, probably-plague-infected rat. I'm pretty sure it was just some local rodent they grabbed up in an alley and went, "Yeah, this one will save money from our prop budget." Being an animal lover, I did not like how these animals were used, even if they were rats, because they taped them up. The crew noticed my concern and assured me the rats would be unharmed and released.

Now the actor—bless him—was a total trooper. He lay there, mouth open, while someone coaxed the rat toward his face. And sure enough, the little guy took the bait and crawled right into his mouth. I mean practically into his throat—and he has to keep it in there for quite a while.

I was watching from off-camera, trying not to scream or laugh. The rat actually scratched his face drawing blood trying to get out of his pie hole. Yep, another savings on prop blood.

I'll tell you what—give that man an award. Or at least a tetanus shot.

If you ever watch that scene and think, "Wow, that rat looks really real,"—it is. Because it was. Hong Kong survival tip: Make sure all your shots are up-to-date.

Dirt in My Face, Just Another Day

Then we shot a truck scene where I'm hanging out the window, upside down, with one leg inside the truck and my face hovering just above the ground. There's a crew guy under the seat literally holding onto my leg with just his hands to keep me from falling out. Meanwhile, Director Yuen Kwai decides to add some flair. He tosses sand into the spinning tire so it sprays directly into my eyes. Ah yes, nothing says "cinema magic" like swallowing dust, dirt and gravel.

The Metal-Armed Muay Thai Showdown

Oh—and then there's that fight scene I do with the Muay Thai national champion. None of the stunt guys wanted to spar with him because he hit too hard. And, surprise! He didn't speak English or Cantonese, so we couldn't even warn each other.

I'm fighting in a dress—no room for pads on my legs. Every kick to my shins felt like someone was attacking me with a steel baseball bat. My forearms? Toast. So the crew made me metal guards to protect my arms. Worked great—until he started getting hurt. So they made him metal guards too.

Now we're fighting metal-on-metal, and every time we clash, it's *CLINK! CLANK!* Like a martial arts sword fight, except it's our arms. And then there's that one scene—you'll miss it if you blink—where he kicks out my leg and I fall flat on my face. No hands, no pads, just pure gravity. Try that at home, and let me know how it goes. Actually—don't.

High Heels of Death

There's a rooftop fight where I'm in heels. Heels again. For three weeks I'm fighting on ladders, running across rooftops like I'm in Die Hard: The Ballet. I'm honestly amazed I didn't snap both ankles, and crawl off set.

But you know what? The action in *Lady Reporter* holds up.

Funny enough, when they screened the movie in England, they gave the audience whistles to blow every time they spotted a continuity error. So every time my hair changed from short to long to who-knows-what, the whole theater sounded like a soccer match. I walked into a room with bangs and came out with a ponytail like Poof! Magic!

But despite the chaos, the danger, the sand-in-the-face, and the multiple "hey-I-could-die-here" moment—and I loved it. It's one of my favorite action films.

CHAPTER 10

PRINCE OF THE SUN

"Through every challenge, every victory, and every moment I didn't think I'd make it, my connection to God gave me strength. It's in that quiet faith that I found the courage to keep going when the world said stop."

Prince of the Sun is a film I really enjoyed, because first off—I got to play a monk. Not your average street clothes gig. No jeans, no leather jacket—just full-on robes which was a refreshing change up!

And second, we were shooting in Nepal, which at the time I had never been to. That alone made it exciting. All the exteriors were in Nepal, and the interiors we shot in Hong Kong—your classic two-city combo.

It starred my good friend Conan Lee? Back then he was being groomed as the next Bruce Lee. I mean, they gave him the hair, the body, even the attitude. But Conan definitely carved out his own path. Also in the cast? The one and only Jeff Falcon—a phenomenal wu-shu martial artist and also the unofficial king of behind-the-scenes drama.

The Monk Robe Showdown

So, picture this: a bunch of us and stunt performers in full monk robes, taking a break from shooting. They tell us, "There's a coffee shop in town." The issue was, we had nowhere to change out of costume.

So off we go—about ten of us, looking like a gang of rogue Shaolin monks on a Starbucks run. We walk into this little place, and a real monk comes over—clearly one of the not-so-peaceful variety. Turns out in Nepal, not all monks are on the straight and narrow. Some enter the life for spirituality… others for the free food and rent-free living.

This warrior-monk starts eyeing us, especially our lead faux monk in the golden robes, and then he loses it. Starts shouting, wants to throw down with us. I'm thinking, Sir, this is a coffee shop, not a kung fu movie —oh wait, maybe it is.

Luckily, there was no epic fight. Someone handed him some money, which worked faster than any prayer beads, and he peacefully went on his way.

The Temple of 500 Monks

One of the coolest things we filmed was at that massive temple—the one with the giant eye painted on it. Such an iconic place. And there were 500 real monks on set. That was our budget—real monks as extras. It was surreal.

The scene where I'm fighting on the pillars was easily the most dangerous. The columns ranged anywhere from three feet to twenty-five feet high. And we were wired up, doing a full fight scene while balanced on these things like mountain goats on caffeine. The guy I was fighting was accidentally dropped mid-scene when the wire guys let go by mistake. He slid down one of the pillars like a cheese grater and scraped his back so bad we thought he'd need stitches.

After seeing that, I was like, "You guys better NOT drop me. I will haunt you."

Jeff vs. Conan: Battle of the Egos

Now Jeff Falcon and Conan Lee had a little friendly tension going on. One day during rehearsal, Jeff's telling me about this movie he wrote—his dream project—and his character's name is "Thor."

Conan just looks at him and goes, "Who the heck names a guy Thor?"

And Jeff, without missing a beat, says, "I don't know, *CO-NAN?*"

It got real quiet after that. But let's be honest, that energy definitely helped the on-screen fighting!

The Wild Boar Disaster

So one night, the restaurant owner wants to treat us. He brings out this big fancy dish of wild boar—his specialty. It's basically a slab of shoe leather with a hint of gamey regret.

We bow our heads to say a prayer—being respectful —and the chef freaks out. He runs out screaming,

"What's wrong?! What's wrong with the food?!" He thought we were mourning our plates or something.

We tried to eat it. We really did. But it was like chewing a rubber tire covered in beef jerky. So we started hiding it—shoving chunks into napkins, bags, even inside jackets. And just when we think we're free…

The owner, who thought we necked this chaw down, brings out more. A second platter the size of a truck tire because we "loved it so much" Ugg.   It was the longest dinner of my life. Moral of the story: Do not eat wild boar in Nepal… just trust me on that one.

The Worst Safari Ever

We had one day off in Nepal. Some people went shopping for rugs—they're famous and super cheap. But me? Oh no. I said, "Let's do something fun. Something wild."

So I found this elephant jungle ride. Five of us go—me, the director, the producer, and a couple of crew members.

I'm pumped and start telling the them that the "safari" includes   champagne, dangerous wild animals, and adventure on the back of an elephant.

The safari kicks off with us on this five-mile-an-hour elephant walking a turtle's pace through some vegetation and I'm thinking, "Can this elephant outrun a tiger? Should I be sipping champagne during this ordeal?"

Suddenly, the tour guide starts yelling, "Tiger! Tiger!" and I nearly spilled my drink all over myself—then I see it—a tiger image on a 2D piece of painted plywood stuck in the bushes. That was our adrenaline-fused safari and for the next six hours we were attacked by several other dangerous cardboard critters. I think we saw one real squirrel the entire trek.

Meanwhile, the other group came back with gorgeous rugs, and a well-rested souls. I came back with a sore butt and four people who wouldn't speak to me.

Rosebush Revenge

I'm filming a fight scene with Jeff Falcon. It's intense, we're backing up in the choreography. And behind me? A massive rosebush with three-inch thorns and a ring of cement spikes.

I can't see it. My foot clips one of the cement things, I go down like a bowling pin—right into the bush. I jump up, screaming, and I can't move.

I had 35 thorns stuck in my butt.

They had to pull me out of the bush like I was a human pincushion. And of course I ran to the bathroom thinking, "Do I need a doctor? A tetanus shot? A new butt?"

Jeff just shrugs and says, "Didn't you see it?" I'm like, "No, Jeff. I was busy fighting you."

The Verdict... *Prince of the Sun* was one of those Hong Kong movies where the action was epic, the locations were stunning, and the chaos was unforgettable. The special effects? Let's just say they were… charming. If you liked *The Golden Child*, this was definitely Hong Kong's spiritual cousin—with more wirework, and less budget.

My hair was doing something weird in that one too. I was in the middle of growing it out, so I had that awkward blunt bob hairstyle thing going on. That wasn't a costume choice. That was just me… fighting bad guys, and demons with a haircut from a department store salon.

But if you haven't seen it—check it out. You'll get monks, magic, martial arts, and a cardboard jungle adventure I'll never live down.

CHAPTER 11

BEYOND HONG KONG ENTER "CHINA O'BRIEN"

"Make change happen. Life's too short not to enjoy every moment—passion fuels success, and joy keeps you unstoppable."

China O'Brien is technically my second English-language movie, and I was so ready for it. At the time, I was still living in Hong Kong, bouncing off concrete and surviving exploding crates on the regular. So when *Golden Harvest* said, "Hey, want to shoot two movies in America in English?" I practically screamed, "YES!" louder than any dubbed villain in a kung fu flick.

I had been in Hong Kong for three years by then and missed the sweet comforts of home—like knowing what my lines were before the camera started rolling. They told me the director was Robert Clouse who directed *Enter the Dragon*. I was excited to work with a legend.

They also told me they were sending a Hong Kong stunt team to help. That turned out to mean two guys, but still a welcomed asset for the fight scenes.

So off we went to shoot in Park City, Utah, where the air is thin, the cowboy hats are real, and the altitude has no mercy. The plan? Two movies in six weeks. Two full martial arts features back-to-back with one meatball per actor. More on that in a second.

Welcome to Utah: Where the Altitude Kicks Harder Than I Do

When we got to Utah, I thought, This will be cake! But what no one warned me about was the altitude. I swear, for the first few days, just walking felt like I'd done 50 burpees. We'd finish a take, and I'd be bent over gasping from the thinner air. Note to self: Spend more time working out in Big Bear, California.

Then came the reality check: we had an actual script. You don't get that luxury in Hong Kong! There, it's more like, "Here's a wig and a machete, go fight those 12 guys." Suddenly, I had to learn lines in advance. But not really, because one day Robert Clouse walked onto set and said, "Let's shoot this scene… from the second movie."

Richard Norton and I looked at each other like, Wait, what?

We hadn't even opened that script yet. Robert just waved it off and said, "Doesn't matter, we'll wing it. I'll just prompt you."

Meatballs and Budget Tricks

This was not a mega-budget film, but it was more of a "guerrilla film disguised as a martial arts classic." And no one embodied that more than our producer, Fred Weintraub—a legend in his own right, and also a budget ninja.

There's a scene where there's a buffet party. Looks like a celebration in the movie, right?

That was actually our cast and crew craft services lunch.

At one point, Richard Norton grabbed two meatballs, and Fred stormed over to him like he'd committed a felony. "Two meatballs?! Richard, if everyone takes two, we won't have enough. Put one back."

Richard's face sinks, and he drops a meatball back onto the pile. Then Richard turns to Fred and says, "Okay, but I'm heading off-set for a couple hours to get some food." Fred relented and Richard got his second meatball.

Heels, Bars, and Multi-Wigged Stuntmen

There's a bar fight scene where I do a high kick in heels. I kicked a guy, and my stiletto got stuck in his chest pad like a corkscrew. I just kept talking, pulled my heel out like it was part of the choreography, and walked off. Nailed it. We all laughed, but Robert Clouse was like, "Nope. Reshoot." I still think they should used that clip.

Also, we didn't have enough stunt people. So one of them wore multiple wigs and fought me, Richard, and Keith Cook—in the same scene. If you look close, you'll see the same guy get punched three different ways with three different hairstyles.

Oh, and then there was the *"prop-cident"*. I guess one of the prop guys missed the memo about using fake glass bottles for the fight scene. He placed real broken beer bottles for the bar fight. A stunt guy was hit in the face and came up looking like a horror movie extra. Real blood, not corn syrup. That prop guy was fired.

When Your Finger Meets Mr. Non-Stuntman

Some of the people cast to fight me weren't stuntmen. They were more like "Hey you, guy walking past set—come fight Cynthia."

In one scene, I had to pull a guy in by the lapels. Simple, right? Except this guy resisted instead of going with it, and *SNAP*—he broke my finger. In the picnic fight scene, you'll see me fighting with a mic in one hand, and I can't make a fist with the other due to the cast on my finger.

The Stallone Film That Almost Was

Now here's the Hollywood twist. One night during the shoot, I came back to the hotel and had a message waiting: *Call William Friedkin*. I thought Richard Norton was pranking me. I quickly learned Richard wasn't playing a joke. I called the number, and a voice said, "Hello. This is Billy Friedkin. I directed *The Exorcist*." I nearly dropped the phone.

He said, Sylvester Stallone wanted me to fly to LA to talk about a new movie called *The Executioner*—and they wanted me to co-star with Sly. Cue me calling my mom: "Mom, Do you know who Stallone is" She says, "You mean that *Rambo* guy?!"

They flew me in on a Sunday (my only day off), Friedkin picked me up wearing a *Bad Billy* t-shirt (no joke), and I met with Stallone, Joel Silver, and the team. They even handed me a contract. I thought, This is it! I'm going to Hollywood!

Then... I learned Friedkin hated the script. The whole project fizzled, but hey—I got paid. It was a *Pay or Play* deal which means I get paid in-full even if the movie doesn't go. Still, I would have loved to shoot that film, even for no pay.

The Sequels That Weren't (Yet)

China O'Brien did great. It was even #2 in the UK, right behind *Rain Man* in video releases. *Golden Harvest* wanted to do part 3 and 4. But Stallone's team stepped in, said "no way," and tried to get me an ICM deal that led... nowhere. Ah, Hollywood.

Final Thoughts: High Heels, Meatballs, and Missed Calls

China O'Brien might've been made on a one-meatball budget, but it's one of the films people still talk to me about the most. It was fun, and unexpectedly emotional. And if you watch closely, you'll see everything: real injuries, recycled stuntmen, and one tough blonde surviving it all with a smile—and a broken finger.

CHAPTER 12

BECOMING THE LADY DRAGON

"The journey to discovering your true self isn't always easy—it takes facing fears, breaking limits, and shedding expectations. But when you finally stand in your own power, that's when you become your magnificent 'you'."

Lady Dragon will always have a very special place in my heart—and not just because people come up to me at airports, comic cons, random grocery stores, and remote places saying, "Hey, Lady Dragon!" That movie gave me the name. Before that, I was Cynthia Rothrock, martial artist-slash-actress. After that? I was The Lady Dragon. Capital "L," capital "D." It's funny how one film can brand you forever—and honestly, I'm not complaining. Could've been worse. "Lady Wombat" but that doesn't exactly scream action hero.

We shot *Lady Dragon* in Indonesia, and thankfully, it wasn't my first rodeo there. I'd already done a film prior, so I knew the terrain, the crew, and more importantly, where to find decent coffee. Working with Richard Ginty was such a treat—I'd admired his work for years, and he didn't disappoint. And of course, my good friend Richard Norton was back for more screen-punching chemistry. You know it's a real martial arts film when Richard gets kicked in the face.

Now, my absolute favorite scene—hands down—was the training montage in the woods. You know, the one where I'm balancing on logs, doing push-ups on rocks, and generally being put through the wringer by the wise old master. It gave me major *Karate Kid* vibes, except swap out the "wax on, wax off" for "don't fall and break your nose." It also reminded me of the old-school Jackie Chan films—using whatever's around you to train. I half expected a monkey in sunglasses to show up and start coaching me.

Not everything was as peaceful as the woods, though. Let's talk about that bar scene. Imagine this: I charge into a sleazy joint, full of determination and hairspray, only to get tossed around, beaten up, and literally thrown into the mud. Not the fake Hollywood kind either—we're talking real, earthy, bug-filled Indonesian mud. After they threw me out of the car and into it, I came up looking like a warrior... or a swamp creature. I had cuts, bruises, mud in places I didn't know I had, and I'm pretty sure I still had bugs and twigs in my hair at lunch.

The fight scenes were the heartbeat of the film. The Indonesian stunt team was phenomenal—fast, skilled, and not afraid to take a hit (or dish one out). The final fight between Richard Norton and me? Let's just say we weren't pulling many punches. It's that Hong Kong rhythm we both enjoy—full-contact dance. Painful, sweaty, adrenaline-fueled dance.

The fashion wardrobe, or lack thereof, was total DIY. We didn't have a hairstylist on set, so what you see on screen? That was me and a can of drugstore hairspray trying to defy humidity. As for wardrobe, I had to go shopping myself. One of the dresses I wore—this wild, gold, sparkly number—looked like Prince's rejected tour outfit. I think I still have it somewhere in my closet, purely for the nostalgia—and maybe Halloween.

Filming in Indonesia always kept me on my toes. One day we'd be sweating buckets under the sun, the next I'd be freezing my butt off in the mountains of Bali. I remember being totally unprepared for the weather shifts—ended up buying a winter coat and a fuzzy hat in a place better known for beach towels and flip-flops.

The movie turned out to be a big hit, breaking box office records around the world, and earning us a sequel. *Lady Dragon 2* brought a whole new level of awesome: I got to work with Billy Drago—the terrifying white-suited villain from The Untouchables. I was nervous. Billy was used to big-budget sets, and here we were with no trailers, outdoor makeup chairs, and asking local villagers to use their bathrooms. But Billy? He was a total pro. He pulled me aside and said, "It doesn't matter if it's a big movie or a small one—just bring your best." That stuck with me.

There's one scene in *Lady Dragon 2* that still haunts me a bit. The one where Billy's character sexually assaults mine. It was intense, emotionally and physically. I told Billy, "Scare me all you want, but don't rip my clothes, okay?" And wow, did he bring the intensity. At one point, he covered my mouth and nose, and I legit couldn't breathe—I thought I was about to become a tragic on-set story. But after the take, he immediately turned into a teddy bear, kissed me on the cheek, and said thank you. That's some wonderful acting.

I'll never forget trying to deliver dramatic dialogue during a nighttime scene, with 200 locals just behind the camera making faces and cheering like we were in a stadium. It's hard to cry over your murdered husband when a crowd, two feet from your face, is yelling "You go, Lady Dragon!"

There was talk about doing *Lady Dragon 3*, and who knows? Maybe someday it'll happen—insert plot here—me battling thugs to get my kidnapped daughter back, kicking my way back through Indonesia to take down a drug lord. As with all my films, other than my latest film, *Black Creek*, I don't own the right to them. Until then, if you ever want to know more about filming in far-off lands with minimal amenities, maximum sweat, and a whole lot of martial arts magic—just ask. Because *Lady Dragon* isn't just a title. It's my survival badge moniker.

CHAPTER 13

FROM ACTION STAR TO PRODUCER

"Taking your fate into your own hands means choosing courage over comfort—and trusting that the strength you need is already within you."

The idea for *Black Creek* didn't arrive with fireworks or a dramatic lightning strike. It came quietly, the way big life decisions often do—through a simple conversation with my partner, producer and co-writer of *Black Creek*, Robert Clancy. One day he said to me, "You should do your own movie."

It was something I'd been thinking about for a long time but never fully committed to. Sometimes it just takes a suggestive nudge to move a mountain. I'd spent decades working in action films, trusting other people's visions, stepping into characters they created. But this time, Robert said, "Let's just do it." And suddenly, the idea didn't feel so far away.

He asked me what kind of movie I wanted to make. He had an idea about a modern action film, but I knew immediately what I wanted.

"I want to do a Western."

He paused. "A Western?"

Yes—a Western. I'd always loved them. But more than that, I'd noticed something missing. You don't see many female gunslingers in films who can really fight. Growing up, I was inspired by legendary American sharpshooter, Annie Oakley—a female superstar from humble beginnings who dazzled the world with her incredible marksmanship in *Buffalo Bill's Wild West Show*. I remember thinking how cool it was that there was a woman in the Old West who could hold her own. I wanted to bring that spirit back, but with grit, toughness, and martial arts woven into it.

From there, the questions started flowing. What's the premise? Is it revenge? Is it family? Is it survival? We talked, brainstormed, and slowly the pieces came together. That's how *Black Creek* was born—a bit over the top graphic novel version of the Old West.

One thing was non-negotiable for me: the women in this film had to be strong. Not the usual Western trope of the damsel in distress waiting for a cowboy to save her. I wanted tough women—bad-mouthed, whiskey-drinking, rough-around-the-edges women. The kind of rolls you usually see played by men. I wanted to reverse those roles and show women in that same unapologetic light.

The character of Rose Jennings is about thirty percent me. She's rougher than I am, drinks more than I do, and definitely uses more colorful language than I ever would in real life. But we do share one important trait—we can fight. Rose is complex. She's not just a tough, silent gunslinger in the Clint Eastwood mold. She loves her family. She feels loss deeply. When people die, it affects her. When she wants revenge, it comes from a real place. I wanted her to feel human, layered, and believable—more than the one-dimensional action heroes we've seen so many times before.

Her look was just as important as her personality. Rose doesn't change outfits much. She wears the same gear because that's realistic. But I wanted it to stand out. We started with an authentic 1800s Western base, then I took it to a seamstress and said, "Let's add fur. Let's add fringe." I wanted something slightly graphic-novel-like—still Western, but with an edge.

I also made some very practical choices. I used a cross-draw holster because it was more comfortable for me. The guns and belt were heavy, and I didn't like anything interfering with my kicking leg. There's a moment in the film where I draw and turn—it just felt more natural that way, even though I'd trained with traditional holsters before.

If you look closely, you'll notice a scorpion emblem on my belt buckle and spurs. That was all custom-made by Roger Halas, a specialty film prop maker who has credits for *Mandelorian, Obie Wan* and *Aquaman*. Years ago, I created my signature Scorpion Kick—the move where I kick backward over my head—and it became something I was known for. I wanted to weave that identity into the film with subtle "Easter eggs." The scorpion imagery, in scenes with the character Xiang, little details hidden throughout the movie—things fans could spot if they were paying attention.

The octagon shaped arena in the film was another intentional design choice and a nod to classic martial arts films. In the Old West, people fought in corrals, but our main villain, Damien Sinclair (portrayed by Richard Norton), sees himself as a Roman emperor. So we blended Western elements with Roman aesthetics. If you look carefully at his office and surroundings, you'll see references to the Roman Empire everywhere. He's eccentric, powerful, and just a little unhinged—and the environment reflects that.

We filmed at *Mescal Movie Set* in Arizona, an iconic Western location where movies such as *Tombstone, Outlaw Josie Wales, Tom Horn* and other stellar westerns were filmed. Interestingly, the corral we built was on the same spot where Harod's house once stood in *The Quick and the Dead*. That wasn't planned—it just felt right for the story and the town. The arena was built so well that it's now a permanent part of the *Mescal Movie Set*.

For the character Xiyang (portrayed by Don 'The Dragon' Wilson), we wanted him isolated, living out in the desert, a loner whose closest companion is a mule he talks to. That separation from town helped define his personality. Don was the only actor I had in mind when writing that role. When I first explained it to him—half Chinese, half Native American, eccentric, talking to a donkey—he couldn't quite picture it. But once he got on set, it clicked. He said, "I get it! I'm the *Yoda* of *Black*

Creek!" Later, after the premiere, Don told me many people came up and praised his acting. "In forty years of filmmaking", he said, "that had never happened before." That moment meant a lot to me.

Some of the character names in *Black Creek* are personal, too. Roy was named after my husky, who literally "barked" the name while we were brainstorming. Katie's name came from my Siamese cat after she walked across the keyboard when we were writing the screenplay. Those little personal touches made the film feel even more like home.

The action choreography was something I cared deeply about. I wanted it to look different. So I brought in two stunt teams—one headed by Mike Möller from Germany and the the other led by Noel Gaylord from Switzerland. Mike Möller oversaw and directed all action scenes. The two teams worked together beautifully, creating something fresh and dynamic. When we do *Black Creek 2*, I'd love them to be on the team again.

And yes—we shot the entire film in fourteen days with a small independent film budget. To this day, I don't know how we did it. It took love, dedication, and an unbelievable team. Everyone showed up ready to give their all. This wasn't just my movie—it was a true collaboration.

Black Creek is also a reunion. Richard Norton and Keith Cook joined me for the first time in over thirty years since the *China O'Brien* films. I knew fans would love seeing us together again. I wanted the biggest martial arts cast I could afford—real fighters, real action, no shortcuts. It's also bittersweet that *Black Creek* is Richard Norton's last film, but I am touched that we got one more epic fight scene together.

One thing to note is this film production was quite different for me. I wasn't sitting in my trailer studying lines. I was on set constantly, watching everything. On the first day alone, we had over 150 people on set—fans, backers, supporters. Many had never been on a film set before. It was freezing—Arizona desert cold, down near thirty degrees—and they stayed outside until five in the morning just to be part of it. That kind of support still humbles me.

Out of *Black Creek* came a family—a real one. We have a *Black Creek* Cast Facebook group where people stay in touch, reunite at events, and support one another. That doesn't usually happen with movies. This one created lifelong bonds.

We even expanded the world into a graphic novel, adding backstory—like how Rose learned martial arts. It gave fans another way to connect and see themselves as part of the universe.

When people ask me my favorite scene, it's hard to choose—but the moment involving the Madam, played by Forbes Riley, stands out. We had planned a big fight, but time ran out on our shoot schedule. What we ended up doing instead worked even better than the original idea. Sometimes the best moments come from necessity.

If I'm remembered for *Black Creek*, I hope it's as a woman who had a vision for a decent entertaining film idea with strong female lead, and brought it to life. Someone who didn't give up. Someone fearless enough to take on something huge and see it through. Ten years earlier, I would have told you I'd never make my own movie. Now I hope it inspires other women to do the same.

Don't wait and don't procrastinate. If you have a vision—*go do it!*

I was blessed with amazing fans on-set, an incredible post-production team led by James Marlowe from Marlowe-Pugnetti Company, Inc., an amazing score by Benjy Gaither, and a powerful theme song written by Legendary Grammy® Award winning, and Oscar® nominated artist and songwriter Jim Peterik and singer, songwriter Marc Scherer. Every piece came together.

Black Creek wasn't just a film. It was pure magic.

ABOUT CYNTHIA ROTHROCK

Cynthia Rothrock is one of the most accomplished figures in martial arts history, dominating competition as a five-time undefeated World Champion in forms and weapons, often competing against men, while earning seven black belts across multiple disciplines. She made history by becoming the inaugural woman to grace the cover of Karate Illustrated (August 1981) and holds the distinction of being the first woman featured on the cover three times in the magazine's history.

Honored as *Black Belt Magazine's* "Female Competitor of the Year" in 1983, she translated her elite skills into a groundbreaking film career after her 1985 debut in *Yes, Madam!* starring alongside Michele Yeoh. She has since starred in over 60 films across Hong Kong and American cinema and has received major honors, including induction into the International Sports Hall of Fame and a Lifetime Achievement Award, cementing her legacy as a true action-genre trailblazer.

- 5-time Undefeated World Champion Martial Artist
- Starred in over 60 films spanning Hong Kong and U.S. action cinema
- Holds seven black belts
- *Black Belt Magazine* Hall of Fame Inductee
- In 2024, *Black Belt Magazine* named Rothrock #1 in its list of "The Most Influential Women Martial Artists on the Planet"
- First woman to appear on the cover of a *Karate Illustrated*
- Featured on cover *Black Belt Magazine* multiple times and over 60 other magazine covers
- *International Sports Hall of Fame* inductee by Arnold Schwarzenegger and Dr. Robert Goldman
- Lifetime Achievement Award at the *Martial Arts SuperShow*

BOY

starring Michelle Yeoh
Cynthia Rothrock
directed by Corey Yuen Kwai
produced by Sammo Hung
Yes, Madam!
皇家師姐

CYNTHIA ROTHROCK
SAMMO HUNG
YUEN BIAO
12
MILLIONAIRES EXPRESS

ANDY LAU
CYNTHIA ROTHROCK
RICHARD NORTON
MAGIC CRYSTAL
A Film by WONG JING

FORTUNE STAR
香港猛片・數碼系列
執法先鋒
RIGHTING WRONGS

NO RETREAT NO SURRENDER 2
IT'S NOT A RE-MATCH...
IT'S WAR!
18
DVD VIDEO
UNIVERSAL

INSPECTOR
WEARS SKIRTS

師姐大晒
The Blonde Fury

CYNTHIA ROTHROCK
PRINCE OF THE SUN
ROTHROCK AT HER FIGHTING BEST !!

From the Producer and Director of "ENTER THE DRAGON"
She Is The Ultimate Weapon
CHINA O'BRIEN

The Director Of KICKBOXER Brings You The New Dragon
She Fights Fire With Fire
CYNTHIA ROTHROCK
LADY DRAGON

CONNECT WITH
CYNTHIA ROTHROCK

Official Website

https://www.CynthiaRothrockOfficial.com

Fan Club / Martial Arts Association

https://Association.CynthiaRothrockOfficial.com

Official Social Media

https://www.facebook.com/CynthiaRothrock
https://www.youtube.com/cynthiarothrockchannel
https://www.instagram.com/officialcynthiarothrock

www.ingramcontent.com/pod-product-compliance
Lightning Source LLC
LaVergne TN
LVHW010929110826
845149LV00013B/2521
* 9 7 8 0 9 8 5 9 3 9 5 6 4 *